Othernatural

Othernatural

Lee Mark Sawatzky

Copyright © 2008 by Lee Mark Sawatzky.

ISBN: Hardcover   978-1-4363-6286-3
              Softcover   978-1-4363-6285-6

All rights reserved. No part of this book may be reproduced or transmitted in any form or by any means, electronic or mechanical, including photocopying, recording, or by any information storage and retrieval system, without permission in writing from the copyright owner.

This book was printed in the United States of America.

To order additional copies of this book, contact:
Xlibris Corporation
1-888-795-4274
www.Xlibris.com
Orders@Xlibris.com
51549

Contents

The Winter of '07	7
a number of primes	10
little bang	13
on poetry (#4)	15
in church today	19
tunneling through	21
I am a Chevrolet	23
don't be late	25
the mighty Fraser	27
a collector of words	29
paying off my motorcycle	30
ol' snakeskin	32
thirty million dollars	35
at transition's edge	39
a religious experience	43
against desolation	45
in the written room	49
differences	52
bad from good	54
tunneling through, continued	56
false spring	62

The Winter of '07

I remember how cold it was
in the Winter of '07,
at the very least it seemed
to get colder, sooner that year

the arrival of the cold
introduced the busyness season
and a developing fear that no activity
would lead to meaningful progress

you know you are too busy
when the things you do blend
into a common, bland mixture,
rendering even the better events repetitive

you know you are getting old
when you realize that,
despite your best caution,
you have been marked by age

you are dented,
scratched, rusty, and dull,
not through and through, but like
an older car someone looked after

you know you are getting old
when you finally understand that
independence means distance
and distance means conflict, yes

you know you are getting old
when you catch yourself
leaning against your porch thinking
rather than continuing to do

(thinking about how love carries forward
for years: love's radioactive background)
even though you know that
what you were doing was probably important

but early on
in the Winter of '07
the thesis, that the world is fundamentally
changed, was almost ready

not changed,
like the difference between
a horse-drawn carriage and
automobile transportation

fundamentally changed,
like the molecular make-up of food,
which looks better than ever
but has no taste

the best ideas we ever had
have been so manipulated that now,
tattered and threadbare, they embarrass
those who wear them

what now passes for great
won't be great later
even though it may have seemed new
. . . the Emperor had more clothes

doing, showing, and telling;
the path
of least restriction
has always been well traveled

this is what I was feeling when
I stumbled once again upon the thought
that good children
sometimes come from bad parents

the unhelped child
can become independent
the harassed child
can become resourceful

so it was that
in the Winter of '07
I prayed against
the cold and the irrevocable change

my God
give me warmth; and please
form what's left of my splintered hope
into the next season

a number of primes

almost every year
I encounter yet another
peak in experience
or ability

one of my most
memorable romances
took place
in fifth grade

I remember
brilliant sunshine blurring
the view through the windows
at the front of the drugstore . . .

. . . as I eagerly carried
the box of chocolate pieces
—they were Nielsen's—
up to the till

but a dozen years sentient
I was overwhelmed
by new feelings of
unprecedented intensity

I probably peaked
as a runner a year or two
after I had stopped
playing sports

in my early twenties
I won a foot race
against my athletic
younger brother

our impromptu
two man race was run
from light pole to light pole
in the cool, wet dark

amazingly,
my fast-twitch fibres
must have continued to develop
without me

looking back,
I may have been most useful
when I taught Sunday School
in my thirties

for fifteen or so years
no one else offered to teach
the ever-changing junior high class
and so I continued on

I refined my teaching
method over the years,
and, in the end,
simply read the Bible out loud

nowadays when I meet
former students I am content
knowing that I strove to respect them
as adults before they were

I had always been impressed
with how quickly
my economics adviser
edited my thesis

in one afternoon the research
contained in a passel of creased,
mix-matched pages went from
almost unrelated to focused

twenty-five years later,
I actually wowed myself
editing a child's university paper
with similar skill

I had lost almost all my speed
on the ice rink, but
apparently as a reader and writer
I had kept getting better

at some point, maybe soon,
my slowing synapses
will fail to keep up with what I chance
to learn each day

if I am witness to that change,
I pray that I will revel
in my new, hopefully more caring,
perhaps grandchildren, prime

little bang

where I live
we are sufficiently comfortable
to take time
to try and understand (full stop)

all of us
enjoy our small-
to-great pleasures
of body and soul

some of us accept
that ultimate meaning, and
the resolution of the great mysteries
rests with God

I've often said
that the problem
of the birth
of the universe

is only a problem
for someone
who does not accept
there is a God

people who don't acknowledge God
have the problem
of trying to explain
how it all got started

according to my observations
anti-God people
are at a loss to decide
what really is important

they appear
willing to mingle
meanings
of very different magnitudes

they treat less important meaning
and lesser mysteries
as being the equal of ultimate meaning
and the great mysteries

for this reason, solving even little mysteries
can prove to be satisfying,
at least for a while:
"I finally figured this puzzle out"

and when the resolution of mysteries
proves elusive, people who don't
embrace God often turn
to the calming images of art

or, they begin the endless study of
one's self—you may have heard it said,
as I have, that such a study can apparently
provide endless fulfillment

back to the Big Bang,
if you can't explain the Big Bang
you focus on
something you can explain

such as what happened
in ever smaller
fractions of a second
after the Big Bang

in the case of life,
if you are haunted
by an inexplicable death
you can, say,

focus on yard work,
or paint a picture
of an old man slouching away
from the village

on poetry (#4)

poetry
conjures up emotion,
place or time, or makes me
stop and think

the best poems are quotations
from a conversation
where there was
an unlimited time to reply

that's from a reader's
perspective,
the outside
looking in

the other
perspective is the poet's,
from the inside
looking out

by some measure
what I write
isn't poetry at all
it's just a collection of thoughts

looking out (from the inside)
poetry tries
to provide
an explanation

sometimes insights
arrive unannounced
before you've thought
about the problem

other times you
write to describe
a joy that
confounds

still other times
the matter at hand
is the faceless
opponent/ally, solitude

solitude forms
with the awareness
of life's
contradictions

contradictions
that can be as basic as
"I don't do what
I have a mind to do

because
I do not have
the heart to carry it
out against myself"

the act of writing
a poem allows me
to feel like I'm responding
in a more permanent way

and, of course,
there is always the fun of coding:
each poem a puzzle
with a hidden message,

the protective cover
made up of ellipses,
metaphors, and Byzantine
changes in theme

sometimes, though,
it seems as if poetry responds
to my solitude almost
without my involvement

as if the real author
is a jazz-worded muse
who is intent on
disregarding my suggestions

if I had a different make-up
I expect my response
to solitude would
be, well, less poetic

if I had a Roman heritage
I could draw upon my *dignitas*
and move stoically
towards what lies ahead

if I were more ambitious
I could dismiss my misgivings,
and re-focus
on the project at hand

if I was more inclined
to fashion I could
remind myself of
my reliance upon design

for me, though,
it is the thinking and
writing of poetry
that helps me to understand

Paul comments on
our powerful ability
to understand our world
in his letter to the Romans

"For since the creation
of the world God's
invisible qualities his eternal
power and divine nature—

have been clearly seen,
being understood from what
has been made, so that men
are without excuse."

perhaps someday I will
endeavor to describe how these
selfsame words
meet solitude head-on

in church today

people who are okay
weren't in church today
only broken people
bothered to show up

most obvious
were the five or so guys
who must have gotten up early
at the recovery house

you see, church starts early,
even earlier when it's cold and wet
that crew must have been pretty low
to have made it on time

they know who they are
and the rest of us
know who they are
but it doesn't matter in church

one row over
and a little ways down
there was a contingent
from grandma M.'s family

S. told me that grandma M.
died early this morning,
which means the family
must have been up all night

I haven't seen grandma M.'s
sons and grandsons
in church for a long time—fit,
young men are not often in attendance

as I looked around it hit me
that today, maybe especially
today, everyone in church
was pretty much busted up

there was a good representation
of the set number of things
that can go wrong: health,
money, relationship, etc.

on my count, within four pews
there was cancer, a failed marriage,
a business setback, and several
missed mortgage payments

all of which meant
that there wasn't anything
fake or distracting
about church today

it wasn't a revue,
or a thought provoking play,
or even a baseball game:
"go angels, go"

it's rare
to find a place
where culture
is so uncomfortable

where worship,
flawed as it must always be,
is so much more real than
any documentary could show

why was I in church today?
a watched sparrow,
I sought God's mercy
as I recovered from a fall

tunneling through

in order to answer questions about faith
I have tried to tunnel through
to the heart of the Christian message
taught to me since my birth

I continually return to John 3:16,
—undoubtedly the first verse
I was asked to memorize—which says
you are simply required to believe

friends of mine who are not steeped
in the Christian tradition
have asked me
what they need to believe in

so I turn to Peter . . .
long before St. Peter's Basilica
and two millennia of tradition
Simon Peter was in the presence of Christ

Christ asked Peter,
"Who do you say that I am?"
Peter's answer
tells us what we must believe

Peter said,
"You are the Christ,
the Son of the living God."
Christ approved of the answer

the power in this belief
is that once you accept Christ's deity
His words are seen as pure truth,
Truth

we all long for meaning
and its senior colleague, Truth
to help guide our
partly formed consciences

not surprisingly,
when we hear Truth
it makes perfect sense
(to test this, consider, first,

the power of the greatest
commandment, to love God,
and, then, the power of the second,
to love our fellow man)

while the requirement of belief
is the Biggest question
next up is the role of evil
which paces restlessly nearby

I am a Chevrolet

I am a Chevrolet
and so I always buy
a Chevrolet

my lineage is the lineage
of a Chevrolet:
to understand me, and the car,
you have to go back
a hundred years ago, or so,
back to when roads
were made of dirt,
oil came from Texas, and
Europeans were resented

back to when light and heat
were the same thing—the light
of a fire, the heat of a fire—back
to when people could pick up
and move to start a new life,
and not just try to start a new life

back to when chrome was the
preferred option and
not just added weight,
to when empty streets
accepted metal fins
and windows were scrunched
in pursuit of style,
to when the most common remark
was you could shoot that
engine and it would still run

today, although it is changing,
what with some of the plastics
coming from here and some of
the metal coming from there,
a Chevrolet is still
a lot like me

Chevy's are made by me,
or rather by people like me,
living in towns like me, watching
things on t.v. like me, with
ambitions like mine, including
even now and again
the ambition to do more than
is expected (but, like me, of course
not always)

why would I ever
buy anything other than a Chevrolet
made by me or by my brother?
to buy something made by someone
else, somewhere would be like using
someone else's arm to turn the key in
the ignition . . . it would be an indictment
of someone like me, it would be an
indictment of me

fast-moving, schooled consumers,
who have forgotten their kin,
assert without a conscience
that automobiles are inanimate chattels,
but they aren't,
they represent us,
they are us, and
I am a Chevrolet

don't be late

win or lose tomorrow, it was a stellar year
for the soccer team affectionately dubbed "la
viola cinghiale" by our Italian guide last fall

(maybe you had to be there, but I still smile
at his jest that we organize the team's
game plan around Roman army tactics)

sharing a soccer shoot-out victory
with a great team is as much fun
as snorkeling in Hawaii

great teams have players
who believe in each other and step forward
when they learn they don't have a keeper

great teams don't give up
on coaches who clearly
don't know what they're doing

players on great teams
smile during practices and at the end of games
no matter how deep they are into a losing skid

now that the year is almost over
I'll tell you what I've learned
and also let you in on my secret strategy

I've learned that speed kills,
you can't coach courage, and
good players don't get caught with the ball

I've also learned you should always pretend that
you're playing a sibling you really want to beat
but who you'd never want to hurt

and I've learned not to look back on a game
when it's over, but instead to immediately
start planning for the game coming up

and, of course, I now realize that fundamentals
win games, you should practice at game speed,
and fitness is either king or queen

it turns out I did have a secret strategy
and, no, it wasn't following Colin's advice
to stop tinkering with the line-up

all year I've tried to coach a different game
(it's funny how these words could be a one line joke
about how little I know about the beautiful game)

the mantra, "coach a different game"
reminded me that soccer can only ever be
one small part of life

and even when
things go horribly wrong on the pitch
the sun will rise and set as usual

never forgetting, though, that like every
other part of life, you get the most out of soccer
by playing it absolutely full on

so, thanks a million for the year, and
if you trust me at all, trust me when I say,
"I treasured your friendships"

you're right, I was joking about that "win or
lose" thing; Starbucks will be on me after the win,
and practice will be on Tuesday

. . . don't be late!

the mighty Fraser

on
several
occasions
this summer
the first thing
I heard from the

                radio alarm by
                  my bed

                                  was an information
                                  bit telling me that a
                                  drop of oil can
                                  contaminate a million
                                  drops of drinking water;
                                  the message that clean water
                                  is so important that we'd
                                  be fools not to avoid polluting
                                  it with oil seems too obvious
                                  (though, the one to a million
                                  does drive the point home)

              in my view, though,
              the much bigger problem
              is that in a good year
              far more than a million salmon

—who not only drink water
but actually live in it—swim
up the greatest salmon-bearing
river in all the world; that river,
the mighty Fraser, is right here
in British Columbia; among this
multitude of fish are many sockeye,
the most prized salmon of all,
who continue swimming up stream
to spawn in the Adams River;
how do we greet these majestic fish

that honour us with their annual loyalty?
we gasoline and diesel-power boat to
our unrestricted delight on the Shuswap
Lake and also on the Adams Lake:
"Have fun friends!" and as a result
each second of each minute of each day,
except presumably a few days in winter,
an untold number of drops of oil mix
with the head waters of the Shuswap
Lake and the Adams Lake and then
mindlessly follow the water's flow down
into the Little River and then down the
Little Shusap Lake and then down the
Thompson River, which in about fifty miles

      feeds the mighty Fraser, that world famous
     river whose mouth is at the Pacific; I fully expect
    to awaken some day soon and hear on my radio that
   a billion drops of oil, or so, did what millennia couldn't
  do: namely, kill the very last fish who began the journey up

the mighty Fraser

a collector of words

I don't want to be a collector of words . . .

. . . or obsessed with austerity,
an observer of fashion always thinking about brand names,
a master storyteller,

or consumed by thoughts of traveling the world,
someone who lives for political causes,
a father exclusively promoting his children,

or inclined to revisit the same set of memories,
a golfer whose handicap is on the way down,
a fearless opponent, a tattoo artist,

or, more broadly, a person lost in the pursuit of any artistic skill,
especially if I start to believe that art—which is often
the most comfortable, consuming interest a person can have—
could very well be, the beginning and end of all things;
you can understand how such a delusion sets in:
just to write down an idea down gives it some significance,
the self-sufficiency of an art form further accreting
around its history, its terminology, and the symbolism
and other types of intelligence visible in better art,

or the world's greatest fan,
an investor with a knack for making brilliant investments,
a researcher on the verge of a breakthrough,

or consumed by a hobby, whether it's restoring a '69 Chevy or completing
a network of scale trains in my basement,
a person known for dedication to his profession,
an irreplaceable teammate,

or a developer with finalized plans for ten acres,
a baker of fruit pies with notable crusts,
a tailor offering a quick turn-around, and reasonable prices,
even a candlestick maker, assuming they still exist . . .

. . . I don't want to be a collector of words if it distracts me from
what is really important.

paying off my motorcycle

Motorcycles are seen as the modern maverick's mount, at least by those that ride them. Young men buy a motorcycle as soon as they can rustle up the cash. Older men have to wait until their children approach self-sufficiency, their careers plateau, and there is an opening on their credit line. Oh yeah, older men also need a few clear days to dream about how buying a motorcycle will re-invent their youth.

I first saw my future motorcycle in a full-page contest advertisement. I hadn't owned a motorcycle for years and I couldn't identify what make of bike I was looking at. The bike, though, seemed to be a good blend of heritage and sport. In short order, and after my brother had assured me there was really only one make of motorcycle, I gave in and bought my new bike. The rest of my story dates from the day I picked it up.

I had agreed to meet a friend at a pub where he was having lunch. My friend didn't know I was going to show up riding a motorcycle. When I arrived, I parked beside an even larger bike. After I had turned off the ignition of my bike, the owner of the other bike—who wore leathers and was obviously more seasoned than I—came up to me in a friendly manner and said, "You're doing it wrong. You always back your bike in." I explained to him that I'd just picked the bike up an hour earlier. We talked a bit longer, after I had re-parked my bike by backing it in.

I went inside to meet my friend. A few minutes later my motorcycle friend came over to our table, smiled, and said, "There are a couple of more things I should tell you. First, remember that from now on you don't have to pay any cover charges. Second, you should take that off your helmet." He then pointed to the bright orange price sticker that was still on the top of my helmet. The joke was only partly on me since I actually never go anywhere there is a cover charge.

Eventually I took my friend outside to see my new bike. As we walked by the bigger bike I noticed it had a sign on it that confirmed, how shall I say this, a connection between the owner and a fairly large, motorcycle-based organization. My motorcycle friend happened to be outside as well. He said, "You know, you really should lose those cords." My old friend looked down at the corduroy pants I was wearing and started laughing. My motorcycle friend continued, "Oh yeah, and if you get some custom pipes people will hear you coming." His final comment, a story really, which I choose not to repeat in its entirety, was a description of how his life changed after he had purchased his new motorcycle; and how I could expect my life to change, especially my luck with the ladies.

I have always thought that these exchanges—which confirmed how out of touch I was (or had become)—were priceless; or, at least went a long ways towards paying off my motorcycle.

ol' snakeskin

who wouldn't want to still be racing
down the sidewalk at the speed
of a young girl
or boy determined
to be on time for a
birthday party or
a pick-up game of any sport

the problem is that
as you age you become increasingly
aware that although you'd like to think
you are still active,
there are fewer things
to pursue, which suggests
you are more ol' snakeskin than snake

when you chance to roll
the memories of glory days around,
like small stones in your hand,
you are reminded
of the developing shortage
of anticipations, few with a character
to rival those of the past

for the person getting older,
the days of today
can be mainly seen
as being made up
of recasts of events from earlier on:
all you see or do is a
reshaping of original experiences

. . . almost without fail, once early each year when
I step outside I become suddenly aware of the unique smell
that signals for me the first day of spring
I usually do not bother to try and differentiate
the confluence of contributing smells,
all heated by the new sun,
that make up the smell of a break in the seasons,
but, upon reflection,
I believe that the smells include
exposed gravel and soil, puddles,
rotting vegetation, and fresh plant growth
interestingly, each year when I first smell spring
I don't think about the spring that is just underway,
but instead I am always transported back
to the springs of my childhood
in my old hometown
many years ago . . .

this is not to say that
there is nothing new in each life,
no matter how old,
or to overlook the comforts
of faith, family, society, beauty,
tradition, etc., and so perhaps
"ol' snakeskin" is too lifeless an image

moreover, weaknesses can act
as strengths; like when the blurring
of memory allows us
to re-enjoy so many things
in a way that would otherwise
become dull: try eating, and still enjoying,
lemon pie for seven days straight

yet, each age has its own neighbours
which, it turns out, are different
from those that populate
the other stages of life, the differences
most pronounced when an
adult contrasts his or her life
with the life of a child

desiring ever greater happiness
won't make it so
likely the best you can do
is to accept that each part of life
is temporary and that in time
you run out of
bigger and better

as you age you may want to
remind yourself
now and again
that you're probably feeling
exactly how you should:
not perfectly comfortable
in your skin, your ol' snakeskin

thirty million dollars

it seems absurd to have to
argue in favour of mom and apple pie
and for having children
but we thought we needed to acquire

the power to carefully plan our children
as a result of the physical law known as "the see-saw
of advances and retreats" which applies to
all mankind's so-called progress

this law ensured that
there would be a cost to pay
for eliminating our predators,
both large and microscopic

because now there would be
too many of us
(I'm told budgies live 10 years in a cage
but only 2 years in the wild)

so I'm not shocked when
a conversation with young adults
rounds the corner on
the benefits and drawbacks of having children

of late, I have started
my remarks with the statement
that my three children are worth
thirty million dollars

I continue by saying
that the largest amount of money
I can imagine dealing with
is ten million dollars

and since each of my children
must be worth that much or more
together they must
be worth thirty million dollars

I then go on to say that
this knowledge has a calming affect
whenever I consider my monthly expenses
and the household debt

(although it is beyond indelicate
to refer to money when discussing life,
I ask for a moment more
to make my point)

your rebuttal might be
that numerous things
—including solitude—
are priceless

and therefore,
according to my standard,
are worth the upper limit
of ten million dollars

I would then respond
that while, with only the rarest
of exceptions, all parents
hold their children dear,

it may be necessary from time to time
to remind society, as a whole,
about the true value
of all of its children

all living things
need to be continually renewed, and who can doubt
but that children are the fresh shoots in spring
that renew humanity

don't think of this renewal
as merely re-stocking
the ranks of the already teeming masses,
no!

think rather of this renewal
in terms of the power
children have to clear
mankind's ever-clouding vision of itself

Christ said, "You have hidden
these things from the wise
and the learned and revealed them
to little children."

He also said, "Whoever
humbles himself like this child
is the greatest
in the kingdom of heaven."

it seems that the simple faith of children
enables them to accept God's love
let me always be with children
seeing, hearing and understanding as they do

the young aren't fatally distracted by their
own importance; instead, they are engaged
by the new beauty of their world
and their bursting lives within it

contrast the fascinations of adults
as adults grow older they focus increasingly inward:
green leaves, turning brown, itemizing everything,
even the processes of their own death

as if by studying yourself even more,
digging ever deeper in your own psyche,
you will be able to uncover some hidden,
ultimate truth about yourself

(I say,
good luck, on being able
to know more
than you can know)

thinking further on it,
I am certain that answers to the ultimate questions
will never be found in weekend editorials
or even books of ideas

rather, I am convinced that many
of the important answers lie in wait near
expressions of love; like when we do
something special for a child

*". . . the boy Peter, already 'father to the man',
can only hope to grow younger still."*

at transition's edge

out here near salt water,
at transition's edge,
there is wave upon wave
of epochal change

big changes track behind
the small changes, which include
graying attendees
at youth events

"We decided to move farther out
when we realized
ours were the only kids
in the cul-de-sac."

"I find that
I have to put it in writing now,
something I never
did before."

"What's meaningful?
I guess the here and now,
and choosing
to rely on people."

who we are and what we believe
seems to have gone
from butterfly
to caterpillar

after the transition
the very last acknowledgement
of our Maker
can be expected to come . . .

. . . from an athlete
who is surprised by his own
God-given talent,
as if watching himself from a distance . . .

. . . or a mother cradling
a dying child,
or a farmer standing alone in drought-stricken fields,
too tired to cry

there were innumerable
stories of private faith
in the face of mystery
in the years preceding the transition

but different stories are told
in a man-made world
where, we think, we control it all,
from stock prices to climate change

basic meanings change too
the phrase "go to hell" now just gauges anger;
and "kingdom come" is a place
to where you are comically blown

so it is when
the fat cat of easy money
(and its companion, a little knowledge)
rubs up against us

from what I see,
economic wellbeing works quickly to subvert
the ideals of the diligent
and anyone else who shares in the happy fortune

and only a bona fide whacko
could argue against
the western world's commitment
not to leave any voter behind

the trick is, you bare a window overlooking purposelessness
when you alter the equation
that God's providence, and hard planting,
grow a garden

social welfare is needed, obviously!
and there's little wrong with expecting as, respectively,
family and citizenry,
inheritances of money and roads

the irony, though, is that each such gift
is as deadly as a seppuku wrapped in holiday paper
which can only mean the first world
will finish last

chrome appliances, a shorter
work week, and a guaranteed early retirement
—freedom at five-five, six, or as late as seven
each a colorful lure with a barbed hook

the premise:
that comfort and predictability
lead to injury or worse clearly has no commercial value
and so stays on the shelf, unsold

but what about the
disorienting chasm
between what people think they are buying
and what they are actually getting?

> back before the transition
> there was a western world that
> is now dismissed as provincial, parochial,
> patriarchal, and superstitious
>
> in that world it was faith
> and family—yes, in that order;
> and in that world often young people chose
> to live other than for themselves
>
> I recently met an anachronistic,
> young missionary couple;
> they were well spoken,
> but had a puny net worth statement

I asked, why did you go abroad
the husband said that he had decided to go
after being challenged to articulate
what he was willing to give up for God

they were both Bible translators
and had met on the field
I asked if there is running water
for them and their children—they said no

it also turns out that there is no electricity,
except for what can be generated by solar power;
and that both malaria and AIDS
are prevalent

I asked them if they felt
they had done some good
they smiled together, and said
they thought so and were going back

sometimes late in the day,
composed and careful-planning
comfort seekers smile knowingly
and refer to "the way of all things"

which means,
don't forget you're all that matters,
but also don't lose sight of the fact
you won't be around forever

during the transition expect the construction
of life-defying casinos
to distract us from the dry rot in
empty church pews and baby rooms

a religious experience

is there a theory
that says experiencing
heightened emotions
provides a life-giving tonic?

our unnumbered emotions
are as different
as plain happy is
from plain sad

the mildest emotions
circle the day to day
of Monday to Friday,
with Saturday off

the strongest emotions
accompany the
events that are recognized
to be important

there is first love
blasting its emotions
of desire, happiness and
continual expectancy

the emotions felt at
a marriage include joy,
anticipation and acceptance
(and possibly fear)

the birth of a child
is attended by parental love,
but also amazement
and interest

on the death of a friend
sorrow is marked
by both sweet and
somewhat bitter memories

an event that
is referred to less often
(if at all), at least in what
I have been reading, . . .

. . . that is saturated
with emotion is
is the worship of God
on Sunday morning

on a good Sunday,
I shed a different kind of tear,
the first tear always
forming in my right eye

my tears are accompanied
by other identifiable
physical reactions, like warm
shivers from my forehead to my knees

thinking on it,
Sunday's emotion includes
feelings of a love of majesty,
acceptance, humility and wonder

as far as I know
I have only ever felt
these exact emotions
on Sunday morning

against desolation

*"For who among men knows the
thoughts of a man except the man's
spirit within him."*
I Corinthians 2:11

it is impossible
to separate the two narratives
that define us: our lives, and our thoughts about our lives,
with emotions somewhere in between

our lives,
as lived out day to day,
would, though, appear to be the primary narrative
as this is what we do and what is done to us

and it would seem
that nothing could ever be more true,
more real,
than our actions and what affects us

the reality of our lives
—which could be called the breathing narrative—
is somehow different from, but intertwines,
the other narrative: our thoughts about our lives

the other narrative is, in part,
an editing room (or a de-briefing room)
wherein we assess each act, whether in the past,
occurring now, or anticipated

the other narrative
must also be the place
where we host
the muse, promoting creativity in all its forms

is the other narrative
our heart, mind, conscience, or soul?
or is it something altogether different?
who knows the complete answer?

the ongoing mystery
of the other narrative
is how mere thoughts
can override our physical impulses

why draw any lines
to limit our animal instincts:
why not always pleasure? what about
the human traits that exceed instinct:

whence love,
altruism,
honor,
being true to one's self?

explaining away the potential power
of the other narrative is an awkward problem
for those who don't believe
there is a communicating God

when you believe there is a God
standards of conduct can be understood as
God-inspired (living expressions of faith)—
which is world's away from the instinctual

if you don't believe there is a God, everything
is arbitrary and it would seem that the only possible reason
to consider your actions are the consequences
that could track through to you or yours

consider
the difference between
loving those who love us, and
loving our enemies

I recently saw an evolutionist on t.v.
explain, in a clammy way it seemed,
that helping total strangers
is consistent with evolution

his explanation was that random acts of kindness
are mistakes ("evolutionary misfirings")
by individuals who confuse the recipient
with someone who can aid them in return

I would never argue
that goodness is the private reserve
of religion-spouting folk,
or that there is not an inclination towards friendship

but I would argue that a certain type of goodness
is evidence of an acknowledgment
there is a God, an acknowledgment
that involves the "other narrative"

if God is not our witness
then surely the breathing narrative
must most times
overwhelm the other narrative

aspiring only to better self,
Nietzsche-like we would connive on,
strive on, subject only to
the broad control of social contracts

live—but don't necessarily let live—
don't second-guess temporary satisfaction
eat, drink and all the rest,
at least until knocked back by the group

if God is not our bread of life
life starts, and has to end, with theses like those of
Sartre ("man must rely on his own fallible will and moral insight")
and Dawkins (evolving animals in a cold, atomic world)

interestingly,
these soulless views
are not generally promoted in our daily interactions,
especially with our children

and they stand in contrast
to the creativity, optimism and hope
we feel
when we are most alive

I have watched rich, godless men face death
they don't need to acquire more wealth
and yet they continue to work
until almost the day they die

when pressed, a rich, godless, dying man
is likely to assert that that he would like to
help set up a family member or leave some kind of mark
—such is self-actualization in the West

if he comments further,
he might say that although his death is imminent
this is what he does to give his life
a daily purpose, which is a form of pleasure

and who can deny that like sharks
who must keep moving forward to survive
we are built to keep doing . . .
doing something

however, I argue against desolation

in the written room

there is
a fairly large mammal
taking up space
in the written room

that needs
to be confronted, namely,
the physical attraction
between the sexes

this powerful attraction
constantly hijacks our thoughts
and manipulates
our ambitions

so, what are any of us
who strive to be semi-pure
—to be somewhat good—
to do?

it's especially tricky
because sex is obviously integral
and our thoughts upon it
corrupt so easily

if that wasn't enough
it turns out that
what we think may as well be
what we do:

"But I tell you that
anyone who looks
at a woman
lustfully

has already
committed adultery
with her in his
heart."

Christ told His followers
they needed
to love God
and love others

it follows that somewhere within love
there must be a defense against
the wanted/unwanted elephant
. . . so what is love?

thinking on it,
love is, in part,
a decision to deny self,
to narrow our experience

my favourite
stories include those
where my contemporaries
chose against youthful temptation

the archetype
of these stories
is the story of Joseph
and the jailer's wife

you may remember,
that Joseph declines
to give in to the sexual advances
of the jailer's wife

this story, and each of the
unique yet overlapping
modern takes,
is a classic story

in a good story,
a believable and powerful
evil contests with a believable
and powerful good

an additional quality
of a classic story is
the uncertainty about the outcome
until the very end

differences

there are some
things you just know;
thoughts that seem
to be worth writing down

thoughts that
you expect to be of value,
perhaps tomorrow,
in an unexpected way

one of my thoughts
is that men are different from women
not to gratuitously frustrate them
but for historical reasons

men needed
to be bull-headed to
protect the cave
or cottage

if they hadn't been bull-headed
they'd have turned and run
at the first sight
of a saber-toothed lion

also, men needed
to be inconstant, flighty even,
to ensure that new lands
would be discovered

Chris Columbus obviously felt
that heading out on a dark sea
was his only chance
to make something of himself

another one of my thoughts
is that there are
irreconcilable differences
between all of us

"I like this more than that"
says the first; the second "likes that"
and the third likes
something else entirely

these differences
mean that people, given enough time,
mostly get bugged beyond measure
by other people,

which makes marriage
—a long term coming together
of two of the most unlike types—
an impossible living arrangement

. . . it is funny, though,
how the durability
of the institution so easily puts a lie
to an otherwise useful thought

bad from good

and yet again
I've learned
what I didn't
think I would

that there is
so much bad
that can come
from something good

imagine
helping someone out,
an act
of altruism,

without
one string attached,
not even
a condition

"good"
that is as good
as ever
a good began

no bad
can come of that!
. . . you would
do well to think again

one thing that
might go wrong
(results can be
contrary)

is that what
you've done
won't fix the
beneficiary

another thing
that can occur
is that someone else,
somewhere

will agree
the gift was helpful
but won't think
that it was fair

"And what
about my gift?"
can sometimes
be their thought

this might
be asked out loud
but usually
it is not

now to finish with
a maxim,
a warning
that is well met,

what comes
from doing good
may not be
what you expect

tunneling through, continued

of course God knew
the consequences
would be beyond
what we could ever understand,

but He still allowed us
to have so much,
the first gift,
to be in His image

I used to think that thoughts and
language were mankind's most
important abilities, but now I realize
how limiting this assessment is

you have to think
as broadly as you can
to comprehend
the glory of being human

what people can do
what people are
the Great books,
the Great emotions

the Great buildings,
the Great adventures
the Great athletes
the Great ideas

the ability to stand up straight,
but it is more than that
it is the ability to split the atom,
but it is much more than that

the ability to care
about orphans
halfway
around the world, and

the ability to begin
to understand an artist's rendering,
but it is still
much more than that

now the trick: coupled to
these almost unimaginable abilities
is the greatest possible
sense of independence and self-worth

Can we fly?
"I'm booked to go to Maui next week."
Can we bring someone back to life?
"Quick, hand me the defibrillator!"

with so much power
we are almost unable
to remember that
we are the created and not the creators

the Greek gods in literature
were given human qualities
because they were us,
and not because we were them

so like those fickle gods
we make decisions
that are not staked out
by any known morality;

some of our uncaring edicts
are insignificant
others, however, are so large
they forever scar our history

the heartless power
of the self-appointed
has an old tradition
on this spinning sphere

going back as it does
to the fallen angel
who knew that knowledge
would allow us to "be like God"

"You said in your heart
I will ascend to heaven;
I will raise my throne
above the stars of God."

when our race
accepted the serpent's recommendation
to take fruit
from the tree of knowledge

the path of humanity
was forever altered
as we were sent out
of perfect Eden

the change was so great
(and seemingly unalterable)
because with this knowledge
we had so inhabited our image,

likened as it is
to God's image,
that we could no longer see
beyond ourselves to God

think well on this
how mere money can distract us
"it is easier for a camel
to go through . . ."

imagine
just how distracting
are our majestic forms
and abilities

God knew that our self-admiration
would have to be confronted
(we would have to suffer)
if we were to remember Him,

and yet He still chose
to create us in this glorious way
and forewent the alternative to make us
something less than what we are

He could have made us animals
who are less able to think and to do
yet He was not swayed
from making us in His image

God knew how this would affect us,
and that it would take
an intervention
of supernatural proportions

to overcome the distorting affect
of our God-like power
and enable us to look past ourselves
and see His glory

the correction could only come
from pain and suffering,
which was, of course,
God's second gift,

> the first metaphor is that God crafted
> a corrective lens to fix our myopia from a molten,
> glassy mixture of chaos, tragedy and pain
> without reference to the physics of this world

        a lens that could only be effective
        when the amalgam included endless war,
        the banality of private evil, an onslaught of diseases,
        and everything that causes pain and cannot be explained

        the second metaphor is God is our combatant
        all-knowing and of unequal strength
        who knocks down those in His image
        not once, but continually, to force us to submit to Him

        knocked down with the realization that some things
        are so horrible that they cannot be explained away
        knocked down with the knowledge
        that we control so very little

to repeat, the great irony is that
this act of love relies on death
(including the death of His son)
and destruction

note that God did not love
all of His creation this well
—contrast God's dealings
with Satan

you see Satan,
who seems to have, like us,
a similar likeness to God,
was not shown the same corrective love

instead, Satan lives the worst
of all lives, untrammeled by earthly setbacks,
he cannot make the long journey
back to the temple of the Lord

you might think it sounds as simple
as God getting our attention
by making us fearful or mad
—"Why me!" (or you, or them),

God knowing
that only when our appetites are unfixed
will we take up more noble thoughts
and remember to pray

however, were we able to stretch
our minds enough
we would realize
just how misguided it would be

to suggest that the God
of the Bible is not affected
by the groaning
of His very creation

The question has always been,
"Why is there pain and suffering?"
There is a far
better question:

"Are we capable of comprehending
even part of God's great love,
a love which can be seen
in both of the gifts He gave us,

the gift of His image, and the gift
of His drawing us back to Him
with pestilence, war,
famine and death?"

false spring

what if
you had to sieve the body
from the soul
to rid worry?

soul (spirit) . . . body . . .
to an onlooker
our human forms must look like
cells under a microscope

each cell the same,
with some variation
in the shape of
each cell's walls

closer up, perhaps our fears
become visible,
and, if so, they would show
as common to us all

worry is a tyrant
whose rule
we only dare ridicule
from a safe distance

not to say that worry
does not, now and again,
relent; the problem
is it always returns

December's warm winds
are a false spring
which do not mark
the arrival of summer

worry, though, cannot
assail the othernatural
as they play games
with different pieces